NATIONAL GEOGRAPHIC

Ladders

NATURE'S GENIUS

Mimicking Nature

by Nancy Woodman

How could you swim as fast as a shark or find water to drink in the desert? Living things, or **organisms,** have the answers to these questions and more. Organisms have amazing features that help them survive.

Scientists, **engineers,** and others are studying nature. They want to **mimic,** or copy, nature in order to solve problems. When they have a problem to solve, they ask, "How would nature do it?"

What problems do people want to solve, and how do they solve them? Read to find out!

Dermal denticles
(magnified)

This swimmer wears a swimsuit
that mimics sharkskin.

Swim Like a Shark?

Athletes wanted to swim faster. Researchers helped them by studying sharks. The researchers learned that sharkskin is made of unusual scales called *dermal denticles*. This skin helps sharks swim very fast.

Then people created swimsuits that mimic sharkskin. The result? In the 2000 Olympics, swimmers wearing the suits won many races. They also broke world records.

A Beak on a Train?

Japan's Shinkansen bullet train is one of the fastest trains in the world. The engineers who created it came across a problem. The train made a loud, booming noise when it came out of a tunnel. Engineers looked to nature for a solution.

A team of engineers studied a kingfisher. This bird dives into the water, beak first. The bird is moving from one environment (air) to another environment (water). Yet it doesn't create a splash. The bullet train was also changing environments (tunnel to open space). This gave the team an idea. The team **designed** the front of the train to mimic the shape of a kingfisher's beak. The result? The train was silent and more **efficient.** It required less energy to run. The team solved a problem by mimicking nature.

Kingfisher

Drink from Desert Air?

Only a few animals can survive in Africa's Namib Desert. The fog-basking beetle is one of those animals. The desert surface is dry, but the morning air can be foggy. This beetle can collect water from the fog.

The Namib Desert is along the Atlantic coast of Africa. Cool ocean air blows toward land. Then fog forms. As fog moves on land, the beetle leans with its head down to collect water on its back. Tiny grooves on the beetle's back move the water toward its mouth. Gulp!

Scientists and engineers observed the beetle and had an idea. They invented the Dew Bank, which collects water from air. The Dew Bank is made of metal. It is left outside all night. By the morning, the metal is cooler than the air around it. Because of this temperature difference, water vapor in the air **condenses** on the metal. This water is called dew. Drops of dew roll down into the tube. The Dew Bank may collect a glass of water a day. This can make a big difference for people in the desert.

Dew Bank

Dome
Water from the air condenses on the cool metal dome. This water is called dew.

Grooves
Grooves on the surface of the dome increase the area where dew can collect. They also direct the dew to the tube.

Tube
The dew trickles down through a narrow gap. It is stored inside the tube.

Cap
People remove the cap, then drink.

Fog-basking beetle

Inside a Termite Mound

Arrows show how air can flow in a termite mound. Cool air enters through vents and flows down. Warm air rises. Warm air can leave the mound through the chimney or mix with the cool air.

Chimney

Channel

Vent

Nest

Fungus gardens

Live Like a Termite?

Termites in Africa live in tall mounds in the desert. They eat fungus that grows inside their mounds. The fungus needs a steady temperature, but the desert temperature changes. It is hot during the day and cold at night.

The termite mounds have a venting system to keep the temperature the same day and night. The termites open and close the vents. Air from outside can flow through the vents.

Builders and engineers mimicked the termites' venting system. When they designed and built the Eastgate Center in Zimbabwe, Africa, they used a similar venting system. The result? The building uses less energy than most buildings its size. And it does not need air conditioning!

Inside the Eastgate Center

Fans help move cool air from the atrium into hollow spaces in the floor of each office. Air warms during the day. It rises out of the building through chimneys. Cement slabs on the outside wall give shade and absorb heat.

Eastgate Center

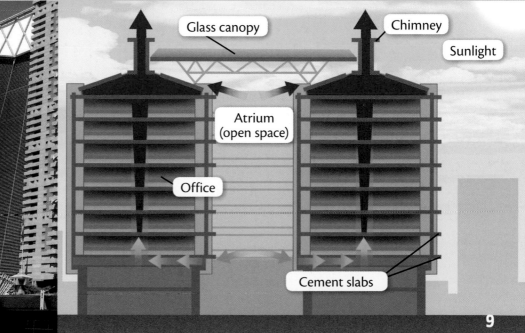

Glass canopy

Chimney

Sunlight

Atrium (open space)

Office

Cement slabs

Bumpy edges make the blades of these wind turbines quieter. The bumps also help the blades spin more efficiently.

Whales in the Sky?

A scientist noticed that the front of a humpback whale flipper is bumpy. He thought that was odd. How could a whale swim efficiently with bumpy flippers? He studied the flipper. He found that the bumps help the whale move with more power. This helps when it is turning.

Engineers used the shape of whale flippers to create blades for wind turbines. These new blades are more efficient and quieter than the old ones. People are also working on parts for more efficient fans and airplanes. The parts mimic the shape of a whale's flipper. More efficient fans and airplanes could help save energy and money.

If you have a problem you don't know how to solve, go outside and observe nature. How would nature do it? What kind of invention will you dream up?

Check In What problems have people solved by studying nature?

Rain Gardens to the Rescue!

by Nancy Woodman

The Problem

In a town or city, much of the ground is covered with roads or other hard surfaces. Unlike grass and soil, hard surfaces can't absorb, or soak up, rainwater. Instead, water flows as **runoff.** The runoff picks up pollutants, like car oil. Most dirty runoff flows into storm sewers. These sewers empty into lakes, rivers, and the ocean. Runoff is a major source of water pollution.

Runoff is the biggest cause of water quality problems in the United States. This is according to the U.S. Environmental Protection Agency.

The Solution

People **designed** rain gardens to reduce runoff. Studies by **engineers** show that rain gardens reduce water pollution, too. A rain garden is a low garden that is dug into the ground. It traps, soaks up, and cleans runoff. The diagram shows how a rain garden works.

A rain garden **mimics** a natural area. In a natural area, rainwater also sinks into the ground. It goes through layers of soil or is taken up by plant roots.

How a Rain Garden Works

Plants
Runoff flows toward the bowl-shaped rain garden. Plants slow down the water and **filter,** or remove, some pollutants.

Pavement

Mulch Layer
Water collects in the rain garden. Mulch is pieces of leaves, bark, or other plant matter. Organisms in the mulch help break down pollutants.

Soil Layer
This layer absorbs water and filters pollutants. Materials such as sand and compost can be added to absorb more water. Roots also take in water and filter, or remove, pollutants.

You can build a rain garden to help keep water clean. Clean water is good for all living things, including you! The water you use every day may come from a river or a lake. Rain gardens help keep that water clean. They trap dirty runoff. This prevents it from going into rivers and lakes. That means cleaner water for you to use.

Some people get water from an **aquifer.** An aquifer is a layer of rock, gravel, or sand below Earth's surface where water collects. Many aquifers are running out of water, but rain gardens can help refill them. Water trapped in a rain garden moves through soil and rock. The soil and rock act as a filter to clean the water. This filtered water may reach an aquifer.

There are many reasons to build a rain garden. It helps refill your water supply and keeps water clean. A rain garden also prevents flooding and can be beautiful to look at. So what are you waiting for? Build a rain garden today!

Check In How can a rain garden help keep water clean?

BIOBOTS

by Jennifer Boudart

A new generation of robots is here. These robots do jobs that are too dangerous for people. Many of the robots look like animals. That's because **engineers** are turning to nature to **design** these robots, or "biobots." *Bio* means "life." Biobots are lifelike robots. Engineers are designing biobots that **mimic** the ways animals move. The biobots crawl, jump, run, swim, and fly. Let's take a look at some biobots!

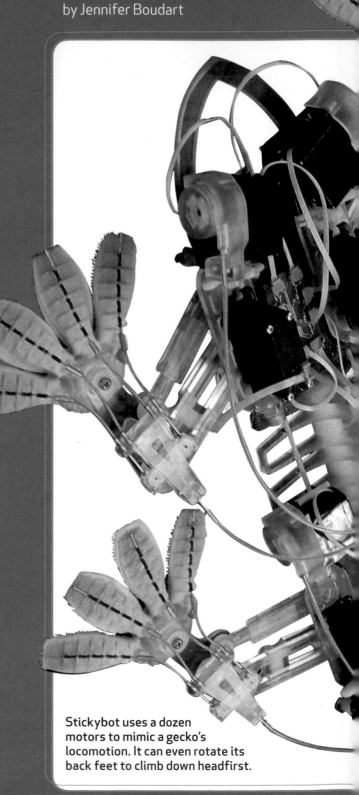

Stickybot uses a dozen motors to mimic a gecko's locomotion. It can even rotate its back feet to climb down headfirst.

STICKYBOT CLIMBS WALLS!

The gecko is a lizard that can easily climb walls. What is the secret to its **locomotion**? It has millions of tiny hairs under each toe. The hairs press down. This makes the toes grip or "stick" to surfaces.

The weight of the gecko's hanging body pulls the hairs downward. This causes the gripping action. Stickybot looks a lot like a gecko. And like the gecko, Stickybot's toes are lined with millions of tiny hairs. This biobot climbs up and down glass and metal surfaces.

Stickybot's foot

Gecko's foot

Stickybot

- **Bio-inspiration: gecko**
- **Locomotion: climbing**
- **Mission: military patrol, search and rescue, building inspection**

MICROFLY
FITS ON A
FINGERTIP!

Microfly

- **Bio-inspiration: blowfly**
- **Locomotion: flying**
- **Mission: military patrol, search and rescue, environmental research**

Microfly is a tiny biobot that mimics a flying insect. It was designed by a team of engineers. They studied the blowfly to learn what makes it an expert flyer. The engineers had to invent small, light parts to build the microfly. This allows it to lift off. Then its skeleton had to be built under a microscope. Tiny mechanical muscles called **actuators** power its wings. The engineers are still working to improve its steering.

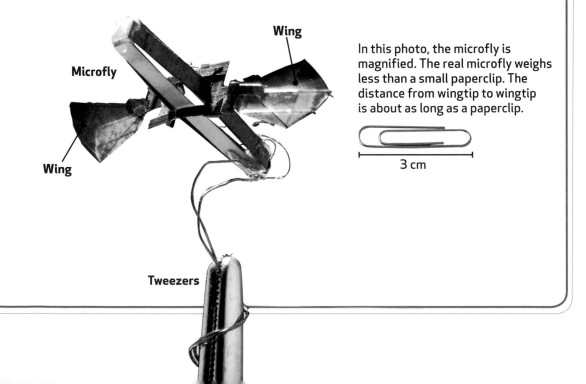

Wing

Microfly

Wing

Tweezers

In this photo, the microfly is magnified. The real microfly weighs less than a small paperclip. The distance from wingtip to wingtip is about as long as a paperclip.

3 cm

Robobee

- **Bio-inspiration:** honeybee
- **Locomotion:** flying
- **Mission:** military patrol, search and rescue, environmental research, crop pollination

ROBOBEES
TO THE
RESCUE!

Wing

Brain
The "brain" processes information from sensors. Some of the sensors are in the robobee's "eyes."

Actuator
The actuator is the "muscle" that moves the wings.

Engineers are hard at work designing robobees. Real honeybees pollinate crops. People depend on these crops for food. However, many honeybees are dying because of a disease. If there aren't enough honeybees, robobees could help pollinate crops. They would use their feet to collect and spread pollen. They might also collect and share information. They might use cameras, minicomputers, and **sensors.** These sensors can detect light, motion, and other objects.

PRECISION URBAN HOPPER
JUMPS OVER
BUILDINGS!

The precision urban hopper looks like a shoebox on wheels. But this robot's sensors can detect tall obstacles. It was built to jump over these objects. Its rod acts like a powerful leg. It pushes down to launch the hopper high into the air. This biobot was inspired by grasshoppers. The precision urban hopper might one day be used to explore Mars or the moon.

A scientist shows off an early version of the hopper. It can jump almost two stories high.

Wheels
Wide wheels help the hopper move over bumpy surfaces.

Rod
The rod moves and then pushes the hopper into the air.

Body
The sturdy body withstands falls from high up in the air.

Precision Urban Hopper

- Bio-inspiration: grasshopper
- Locomotion: rolling, jumping
- Mission: military patrol, search and rescue, space exploration

Robolobster

- **Bio-inspiration: lobster**
- **Locomotion: crawling**
- **Mission: explosives location, pollution tracking, sea life research**

Legs

Nimble legs help the robolobster move around obstacles.

Sensors

The robolobster has sensors for sight, smell, and sound. The sensors detect chemicals, metal, and explosive objects.

ROBOLOBSTER IS A SUPER SNIFFER!

Batteries

Batteries in the robolobster's body provide power.

A lobster can crawl along the seafloor. It has multiple legs. Its sensitive antennae can smell food it cannot see. A biobot called a robolobster looks like the real thing. It has a shell, a tail, and many legs. It has antennae that detect chemicals. These biobots might someday be used to find pollution or underwater mines.

Robolobsters are about 60 centimeters (about 2 feet) long. They weigh about 3 kilograms (about 7 pounds).

FISHBOTS
FOLLOW THE
LEADER!

Fishbot

- **Bio-inspiration: fish**
- **Locomotion: swimming**
- **Mission: marine research, sea life protection**

Swimming in schools helps fish survive. Each fish swims close to its neighbors. The whole school moves as a single unit. If one fish changes direction, the others quickly follow it. This helps fish escape danger or find food.

A fishbot mimics a swimming fish. Engineers' tests have shown that fish treat fishbots as if they're real. Engineers hope fishbots can get schools of fish to follow them. Then they can guide fish away from an oil spill or other dangers.

Fishbots are powered by batteries. They are guided by remote control.

Covering

The covering is flexible
and waterproof.

Tail

The tail moves back
and forth, mimicking
a real fish.

MODSNAKE CAN SLITHER AND SEARCH!

Snakes have a special form of locomotion. They slither and slide. Biobots have been designed to mimic snakes. They are called modsnakes. Uncle Sam is a modsnake. It can wiggle sideways, slip through pipes, roll like a hoop, and climb a tree.

Uncle Sam's head has a camera and a flashlight. Its body is a chain of parts. The parts are linked like train cars. Each part has sensors and actuators. They feel the ground and control movement.

Engineers hope modsnakes can be used to locate and rescue people who are trapped. Modsnakes might also be used to inspect small or dangerous places.

Modsnake

- **Bio-inspiration: snake**
- **Locomotion: slithering, rolling, climbing**
- **Mission: military patrol, search and rescue, inspection**

Head

A camera and flashlight are built into the modsnake's head. A speaker and microphone might be added. Then the modsnake could deliver messages in search and rescue missions.

Links

The body is made of links. Links can be added to make the body longer. They can be removed for repair.

This red, white, and blue modsnake is named "Uncle Sam."

BIGDOG CARRIES HEAVY LOADS!

Engineers studied the locomotion of four-legged animals, too. They designed BigDog. This biobot was designed to transport heavy loads. Its body has a gas tank, motors, a computer system, and sensors. These sensors keep it from tripping. A new version of BigDog is being developed. This biobot, LS3, will be stronger and will use less fuel than BigDog.

BigDog

- **Bio-inspiration: goat, horse, dog**
- **Locomotion: walking, trotting**
- **Mission: military gear transport**

Springs, joints, and many other parts help BigDog move.

Cheetah

- **Bio-inspiration: cheetah**
- **Locomotion: running**
- **Mission: military fighting, emergency response**

CHEETAH OUTRUNS HUMANS!

The cheetah is the world's fastest land mammal. A cheetah's body is built to move fast and turn quickly. Cheetahs inspired a biobot of the same name. This biobot will look a lot like the real thing. Just like the cheetah, it will move fast and turn quickly. It may even be able to outrun humans.

This image shows features that mimic a real cheetah's, such as joints, eyes, and ears.

iSPRAWL
MOVES LIKE A
COCKROACH!

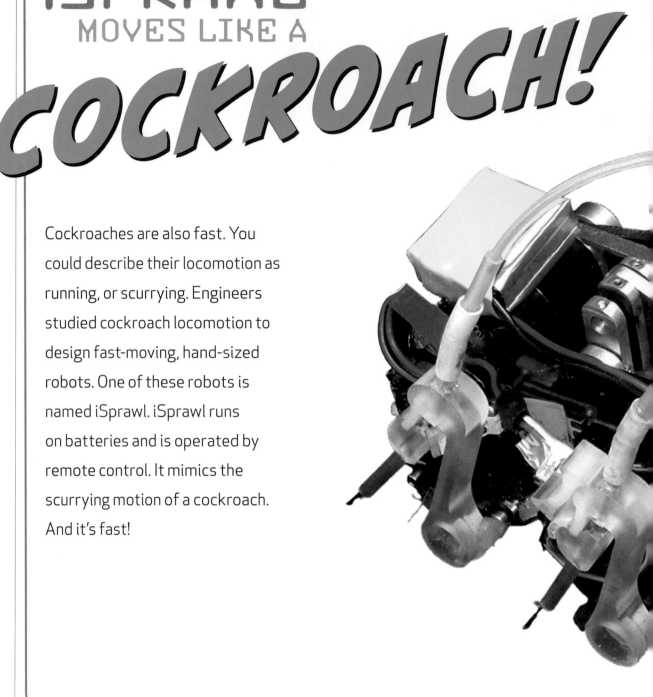

Cockroaches are also fast. You could describe their locomotion as running, or scurrying. Engineers studied cockroach locomotion to design fast-moving, hand-sized robots. One of these robots is named iSprawl. iSprawl runs on batteries and is operated by remote control. It mimics the scurrying motion of a cockroach. And it's fast!

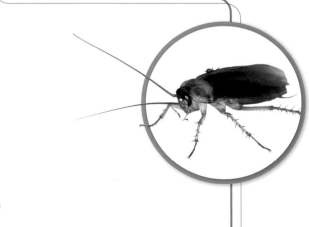

iSprawl

- **Bio-inspiration: cockroach**
- **Locomotion: running**
- **Mission: military patrol, environmental research, search and rescue, space exploration**

Engineers study nature looking for new ideas for biobots. They are wise to mimic what works in nature. There are many life forms to study, so we may see more biobots in the future!

iSprawl can skitter over obstacles as high as tables.

Check In   Which biobot would be most useful to you? Why?

Discuss Explain Ideas, Problems, and Solutions

1. What are the three pieces in this book about?

2. Where did the engineers, scientists, and others get the ideas to make the things described in this book?

3. What problem does a rain garden help solve? Compare it to a problem solved by an invention in "Mimicking Nature."

4. Compare "Mimicking Nature" and "Biobots." How are the inventions described in these two pieces alike and different?

5. Think about what you read in *Nature's Genius*. What do you still wonder about? What else would you like to find out?